The 1981 Pere Marquette
Theology Lecture

CATHOLICS IN THE
PROMISED LAND
OF THE SAINTS

by

JAMES HENNESEY, S.J.

Professor of the History of Christianity
Boston College

Marquette University Press
Milwaukee, Wisconsin 53233

Library of Congress Catalog Number 810309
ISBN 0-87462-536-X

PREFACE

The 1981 Pere Marquette Lecture, twelfth in a series since the Tercentenary Celebration of the missions and explorations of Pere Jacques Marquette, S.J. (1637-1675), also marks the Centennial Celebration of Marquette University, which opened its doors as Marquette College in the Fall of 1881. The Marquette University Theology Department, founded in 1952, launched these annual lectures by distinguished theologians under the title of The Pere Marquette Lectures in 1969.

The 1981 lecture was delivered at Marquette University on April 5, 1981, by Rev. James Hennesey, S.J., Professor of the History of Christianity at Boston College.

Father Hennesey, born in Jersey City, N.J., in 1926, entered the New York Province of the Society of Jesus in 1943 and was ordained in 1957. He received his B.A. from Loyola University of Chicago in 1948, Ph.L. and S.T.L. from Woodstock College in Maryland in 1951 and 1958 and M.A. and Ph.D. in history from the Catholic University of America in 1960 and 1963. Since 1977 he has been Professor of the History of Christianity in Boston College's

Theology Department. He had taught at Fordham University (1962-1971) and in the Graduate Theological Union, Berkeley, California (1971-1973) before becoming President of Jesuit School of Theology in Chicago (1973-1976). He has twice been Visiting Professor of American Church History at Rome's Pontifical Gregorian University and has been Visiting Professor at the University of Chicago, Stanford University, Union Theological Seminary in New York and Memorial University of Newfoundland. His publications include *The First Council of the Vatican: The American Experience* (1963), over ninety articles in the fields of American and modern European religious history and chapters contributed to seven books. A major work, *American Catholics: A History,* is scheduled for publication by Oxford University Press in Fall, 1981. Father Hennesey is currently working on a study of United States-Papal relations, 1790-1870, for the German *Päpste und Papsttum* series and is editing a volume of essays to mark the 175th anniversary in 1983 of the diocese of Boston. He is a member of the editorial boards of *Thought* and *Church History.*

CATHOLICS IN THE PROMISED LAND OF THE SAINTS

By Way of Introduction

Marquette's Theology Department set no small task when they decided the theme of the 1981 Pere Marquette Lecture. The speaker—and there have been times during this past year when I wondered in what dreadfully weak moment I allowed it to be me!—was asked to address himself to a modest little topic: "A Catholic Theological Response to American Civil Religion in a Centennial Year." That mouthful has to be taken, as they used to say—and perhaps still do—in scholastic philosophy, "by parts," in bite-sized portions.

The Centennial

The centennial, of course, is of the September day in 1881 when a brave cohort of seventy-seven youngsters first made the acquaintance of Father Joseph F. Rigge, President, Prefect of Studies and Professor of German at the grandly named Marquette College. Knowing the ways of colleges, there is every chance, however, that the first Jesuit the new students met was Father Michael Cornely. He was the Treasurer. Once he had arranged to collect the annual tuition of sixty dollars—for everything, including stationery—Father Cornely doubled as Professor of Second Grammar in the Commercial Course. He also taught German and Penmanship. By January, 1882, he had organized Marquette's first spiritual organization, the Sodality of the Blessed Virgin Mary. There was no Theology Department.[1] Anyone interested in the real, as opposed to the mythic, history of Jesuit colleges must accept the fact that in them religious influence was of set purpose exercised far more on the practical, devotional side than it was on the intellectual. Philosophy and classics were the principal and integrating academic disciplines, and it had to be treated as a temporary aberration that a majority of Marquette's first students enrolled in the Commercial and not in the Classical Course. Only decades later, in our time, did theology reach beyond apol-

ogetics and by then with only faint hope
of occupying the integrative slot. The all-
pervasive model was that hammered home
by Marquette's ex-President, Herbert C.
Noonan, S.J., when he declared in 1924
that "our moral pre-eminence is our great-
est asset." Father Noonan's favorite image
was that of the "Jesuit in the watchtower,"
although he had to admit that in those
early Roaring Twenties, there were those
who "cowered in cyclone cellars." Mixing
the metaphor in grand style, he urged that
such laggards be extricated from their cellars and retired to duty "behind the firing
line."[2]

Moralism, Devotionalism and Jesuit Presence

Marquette's opening in 1881 climaxed
a quarter-century of effort on the part
of Father Stanislaus P. Lalumiere, the
Hoosier lawyer-turned-priest who had
been sent to Milwaukee in 1857 with
orders "to start an academy and then go
higher when circumstances justified the
undertaking."[3] The college he founded
placed heavy emphasis on the classical

tradition. In philosophy, special attention was paid to logic. The ability to "think clearly" was a prized goal. The Jesuit tradition in moral theology has always been one of cautious, realistic optimism about human nature and its possibilities. That did not prevent instruction in ethics that was clear, precise, firm and unambiguous. The devotional life of the student body was perceived as central, not accidental, to the overall life and purpose of the institution. Father Cornely's Sodality was a key stone in Marquette's beginning. So was the notion of a physical and very obvious Jesuit presence, most vigorously represented by three young men still in their twenties who rounded out the five-man faculty. They were Jesuit scholastics, members of the order studying for the priesthood. Unlike the two priests, respectively a Westphalian and a Luxemburger, the scholastics came of a new generation of American Jesuits. Francis B. Cassilly was from Louisville; James D. Foley and William J. Wallace were Cincinnatians. Classics and philosophy, moralism, devotionalism and a visible Jesuit presence, all these were elements as Marquette's centennial experience began. So was the bishop.

John Martin Henni (1805-1881)

If Lalumiere was the Father of Marquette, the honorable title of godfather surely belongs to the remarkable man who became in 1843 the first Bishop and in 1875 the first Archbishop of Milwaukee, John Martin Henni. He came to the United States as a young seminarian from the Swiss canton of Grisons, a land of glaciers and Alpine peaks and valleys bordering Austria and Italy. His canton was one where languages—German, Italian, Romansh—and religions—Calvinist, Catholic —mingled. Henni turned out to be a man and bishop who personified the genuinely liberal Christian ideal in an age scarred on the one hand by the wretched illiberalism of so many contemporary liberals and on the other by the reactionary conservatism that masqueraded with appalling success as authentic Catholic tradition.

Henni's credits are many. A century and a half ago he fostered bilingual education to ease entry into American society for that generation's refugees. His concerns included catechetics, church music, parochial schools and adult education. He founded three newspapers and sponsored several more. The Church's intellectual dimension was important to him. He was an educated bishop; he wanted an educated clergy and laity. St. Francis Seminary and Marquette College were the result. He promoted equality and tolerance. He opposed alike slavery and prohibition. Neither American Knownothings nor German Forty-Eighters cowed him. In a diocese that the twentieth-century codeword would classify as "ethnic," John Martin Henni was an example in theory and practice of the way in which Catholic can be related to American. The centennial of his death coincides with the centennial of Marquette University's birth. He died on September 8, 1881, two days after the college opened. Its founding had been his dream for over thirty years.[4]

The Promised Land of the Saints

It is tempting to base an analysis of the Catholic experience of America on the subsequent realization of the dreams of Henni and Lalumiere, to follow the first five bachelors of arts to their graduation in 1887, and to meet Daisy Grace Wollcott, B.S., when in 1909 she became the first alumna ever of any Jesuit university anywhere. It would be interesting to determine which of Father Noonan's Jesuits were in the watchtowers and which in the cyclone cellars. But that must be someone else's task. In my part of the world we don't even have cyclone cellars! I should rather like to talk with you under another and broader rubric about the topic proposed by the Theology Department's Père Marquette Committee. Before ever there was an America, Catholics were fascinated, as we shall see, by the lure of "the Promised Land of the Saints." I should like to share with you my curiosity as to how they have fared in the *Righteous Empire,* the *Kingdom of God in America, God's New Israel,* the *Christian America* of *Protestant Hopes and Historical Realities,* the *Nation with the Soul of a Church,* the "Citty upon a Hill" of which Governor John Winthrop wrote while bobbing about

in *Arbella* in the swells off Cape Cod one
early June day in 1630.[5]

The Navigatio Sancti Brendani Abbatis

"Catholics in the Promised Land of the
Saints." The title is borrowed from a tenth-
century manuscript, *The Voyage of St.
Brendan the Abbot*. With a baker's dozen
of fellow adventurer-monks, Brendan
sailed the Atlantic for seven years in a
curragh, a boat of oak-tanned oxhide
which Samuel Eliot Morison termed "little
more than a big wicker basket covered
with skins." Brendan's adventures were
marvelous. There were picnics on the
broad back of Jasconius the whale, who
objected only when the monks lit a fire
there—being Irish, probably to brew their
tea. They met Judas Iscariot, marooned on
a desolate rock and nightly tormented by
little visiting devils from a neighboring
volcano. They had a more pleasant en-
counter with Lucifer's fallen angels, who
on Sundays and holy days were trans-
muted into Latin-speaking birds and gath-
ered for choral recitation of the liturgical
hours. Brendan's medieval seascape is a

tempting place to linger for a bit. But the
point of it all, and the excuse for the pur-
loined title, is that he and his band sailed
the seas in search of the "Promised Land
of the Saints," the *terra repromissionis
sanctorum* which lay beyond the western
horizon. It was a land of fruit and flowers.
A prelude to it was a "delicious island"
peopled by monks, their favorite kind of
people. The Promised Land of the Saints
was something else also. It was a refuge
God had prepared for Christians against
the day of persecution, a land of promise
and of sanctuary.[6]

The *Navigatio Sancti Brendani Abbatis*
and tales like it set the tone of transatlantic
European migration. For our purposes it
does not really matter whether the Vikings
reached Newfoundland or whether there
were Welsh-speaking Indians around
Mobile Bay or whether Brendan and his
monks visited North America and thought
it was the Promised Land of the Saints.
The myth, however, was all important. In
all those stories—legends or histories—the
central core remained: the *Abendland*, the
evening-world beyond the horizon, was a

place of newness and life, of challenge and opportunity. That was true long before Europe's religious revolution in the sixteenth century. It is fascinating, if idle, to speculate how the myth of the Promised Land of the Saints might have taken flesh had John Cabot's voyage in 1498 for King Henry VII of England led to the first permanent English settlement in the New World, or if Verrazano's explorations had directed French settlement to the mouth of the Hudson rather than to the St. Lawrence and the Gulf of Mexico. But in fact neither Catholic England nor Catholic France shaped the mainstream of American colonization. The Promised Land of the Saints turned out to be the Puritan "God's New Israel," and then the secular land of Manifest Destiny.

Civil Religion

Americans have historically understood themselves in terms redolent of Israel's covenant with God. Debate is endless on the precise religious content of the imagery employed and on the extent to which it has been diluted or converted to secular purpose as the "Christian America" postulated by Robert Handy described its arc from days of colonial establishment to the point when "the Protestant era in American life had come to its end by the mid-[nineteen] thirties."[7] In our present context we must ask whether what is Catholic is, and has been, compatible with the values, the symbols and the rituals which have been institutionalized as (the phrase is Michael Novak's) "the cohesive force and center" of the nation.

Ambiguities are everywhere. What is, has been, "Catholic?" What is the precise religious content of the images? What title exists to their ownership? Is it shared? For some, Protestantism, particularly in its Nonconformist expression, and Americanism are nearly convertible. Beyond the words, has it been all that clear? Is emphasis on the dignity of the individual peculiarly Protestant? Or Christian egalitarianism? De Tocqueville thought the latter peculiarly Catholic.[8] What, *pace* Leo XIII and his condemnation of Americanism, of activism? Or moralism? Herbert Noonan was hardly the only Catholic with

firm ideas along that line. Was Philip
Schaff right in 1855 to claim that in the
wake of the Reformation, "with the universal priesthood comes the universal king-
ship?" He argued from there to the con-
geniality of sovereignty of the people with
New England's Puritan oligarchy, at least
on a theoretical basis.[9] Was that a door
closed to Catholics until Vatican II and
Lumen Gentium opened it?

Answers become easier when the case
is simplified. We can recognize the con-
fusion of religion and civic piety when
unbalanced nationalism verges toward
idolatry of the state. The same is true if
the object of cult is the "American Heri-
tage" or the "American Way of Life."
Catholics have been and are prey to such
idolatries. Dorothy Dohen long ago wrote
a book about much of that.[10] When we
talk of that "understanding of the American experience in the light of ultimate and
universal reality," the "genuine apprehen-
sion of universal and transcendent religious reality as seen in or, one could almost say, as revealed through the experience of the American people," out of which

Robert Bellah developed his ideas on civil religion, the situation is more delicate.[11]

For Bellah, civil religion is normative, prophetic reality, the canon by which society's institutions, civil and religious, are measured. It is keyed to concern for equality and inalienable rights. Mary L. Schneider has pointed out that churches abdicate their inherent prophetic function and violate their own integrity if they accept relegation, as Bellah would have it, to the regions of personal piety and voluntary social action.[12] She has also reminded us of those principles "structural to the Western Christian political tradition" recalled by John Courtney Murray:

> . . . the idea that government has a moral basis; that the universal moral law is the foundation of society; that the legal order of society—that is, the state—is subject to judgment by a law that is not statistical but inherent in the nature of man; that the eternal reason of God is the ultimate origin of all law; that this nation in all its aspects—as a society, a state, an ordered and free relationship between governors and governed—is under God.[13]

We have not as a nation sunk to the pure voluntarism of law-as-will and its consequence in unfettered majority rule. The medieval intellectualist tradition survived and found its way into our foundation scriptures. It has a critical role not dissimilar to the one Bellah posits for civil religion. Its phrasings are more congenial to the traditionally trained Catholic mind.

The Heritage Claimed

American Catholics have not been unaware of their medieval legacy. Ninety-seven years ago, speaking in accents remarkably like those of the generation's premier Catholic apologist, Isaac Hecker, the bishops of the Third Plenary Council of Baltimore forcefully rebutted the charge that they and their co-religionists were compromised by a double allegiance, "the assertion that we need to lay aside any of our devotedness to our Church, to be true Americans; the insinuation that we need to abate any of our love for our country's principles and institutions, to be faithful Catholics." "A Catholic finds himself at home in the United States," the bishops insisted, "for the influence of his Church has constantly been exercised in behalf of individual rights and popular liberties." They enunciated their understanding, rooted in their religious belief, of what civil society is all about. From the basic thesis that "there is no power but from God," a series of consequences followed: ". . . back of the events which led to the formation of the Republic, [the Catholic Church] sees the Providence of God leading to that issue, and back of our country's laws the authority of God as their sanction."[14]

There has certainly been a train of thought within American Catholicism convinced of the church's compatibility with our historic democratic institutions. Isaac Hecker and the bishops at Baltimore made them out to be best friends. The 1884 joint pastoral letter not only declared that a Catholic finds himself at home in the United States, but claimed that "the right-minded American nowhere finds himself more at home than in the Catholic Church." Fourteen years later, in the heat of the Spanish-American War, Monsignor Denis O'Connell wrote from Rome to Archbishop John Ireland that it must be "on with the banner of Americanism, which is the banner of God and humanity." The "meanness & narrowness of old Europe" would be replaced by the "freedom & openness of America." "This," O'Connell pontificated, "is God's way of developing the world."[15] Josiah Strong could hardly have said it better. Lost in the euphoria over Manila Bay were the more lugubrious thoughts which, several years before his death, Orestes Brownson had addressed to Isaac Hecker in the late summer of 1870:

> I defend the republican form of government for our country because it is the legal & only practicable form, but I no longer hope anything from it. Catholicity is theoretically compatible with democracy, as you and I explain democracy, but practically, there is, in my judgment, no compatibility between them. According to Catholicity, all power comes from above and descends from high to low; according to democracy all power is infernal, is from below, and ascends from low to high. This is democracy in its practical sense, as politicians & the people do & will understand it. Catholicity & it are mutually antagonistic as the spirit & the flesh, the Church and the World, Christ & Satan.[16]

Catholics in the Promised Land

How then have Catholics fared in the Promised Land of the Saints? Brownson and Hecker, companions for thirty years in religious pilgrimage, ended in substantial disagreement on the question. William A. Clebsch several years back suggested his opinion of the Catholic validity of the "Americanists'" views when he dismissed them as singing "the current songs of the middle-class denominations: progress, social reform and shared religious traditions," songs with the typical refrain, "Thy Kingdom come, in America, *now*."[17] What then was the story of Catholics in the Promised Land? Introducing his reprise on civil religion, *The Broken Covenant,* Robert Bellah announced the wish "to examine the history of America's self-understanding, the myths that have developed to help us interpret who and what we are in America and to inquire whether they may still have power to help us understand our present situation and know how to deal with it."[18] How have Catholics related to America's self-understanding and to its

myths? What help can they find there, or
in other myths of their own?

The Phenomenon

A two-volume study of the Catholic
community's history in the United States
should not be attempted. There is no con-
venient place at which to divide that history evenly. The division traditional in
American histories, at the Civil War, just
will not do. The events of the years 1860-
1865 did not mark a significant turning-
point in the Catholic community's history
here. Catholic soldiers fought, a few
Catholic generals led, and Catholic sisters
nursed on both sides. When the war ended,
Catholic slaves were freed. The church's
leaders, many of them, in the north as well
as in the south, were ideologically on the
losing side. A substantial number of their
parishioners were still angry that the full
promise of America was not yet theirs.
Some showed that in incidents like the
week of Draft Riots in New York City in
the summer of 1863. Still in the Catholic
future were the indignities of the A.P.A.,
the K.K.K. and the P.O.A.U. The Civil

War was not for them a watershed or a
liberation or a welcome.

Two Watersheds and Three Divisions

Catholic American history shares some
of the standard landmarks that have
marked the nation's progress, although it
did not always pause full in front of them.
It has other landmarks more properly its
own. Its mythic history is peopled more by
Hennepin at Niagara Falls and Marquette
and Joliet on the Mississippi than by the
Standishes of Plymouth, the Winthrops of
Charlestown or the Mathers of Boston's
North End. We know a great deal about
Columbus and the help he got from
Spain's Catholic Majesties. Isaac Jogues
holds an honored place, and so do Eusebio
Kino and Junípero Serra and those count-
less Spaniards who sought El Dorado and
the Seven Cities of Cibola. The continuing
history of the Catholic community in the
United States began with a public mass
on the feast of the Annunciation, March
25, 1634, on St. Clement's Island in the
Potomac River. That is our Plymouth Rock
and our Jamestown, along with the origi-

nals. In a corporate sense, the Maryland peninsula washed by the Potomac and the Patuxent is the land where our fathers died.

Most of the first American Catholics were English men and women. They came out under the patronage of an Englishman, Lord Baltimore. Their body included blacks. Mathias Sousa and another man named Francisco were among them almost from the beginning. They were slaves. Increasing numbers of Irish came, nudged along by the loving hands of William and Mary's friends in their native land. Many of them were indentured servants and they were the object of a special tax. Others, like the several families of Carrolls, belonged to the gentry. Pennsylvania had the most mixed colonial Catholic population, German and Irish in the city, heavily German in the country districts. Overall, the colonial and federal Catholics were conservative people. Politically they were Federalists and then Whigs. Some few served the crown during the American Revolution; more were patriots. They had a stunning record for promotion of religious liberty. Wherever, and for as long as, they held power, religious toleration was general. That was true in the earliest part of Maryland's history and confirmed by act of the Maryland assembly in 1639. Only with the advent of Puritans do restrictions like those evident in the 1649 act of toleration appear. New York knew religious liberty under Catholic Governor Thomas Dongan from 1683-1689, and so did Virginia's Northern Neck, on the 1687 petition of Catholic Captain George Brent.

In the first phase of internal post-Revolutionary organization, John Carroll, who became Mission Superior in 1784 and Bishop in 1789, made serious efforts to indigenize Catholicism in its American setting. The clergy organized collegially, complete with a rule of life, common ownership of church property, control of which was kept separate from spiritual power, and an arbitration and conciliation process. They argued their right to select their own bishop. Plans were laid to build a native clergy. Lay people had leadership roles in the colonial church and these continued under independence. Trustees formed themselves into boards and bought or built churches. John Carroll declared that, once canonical parishes were set up, proper regard would be had to the rights of the congregation in the selection of pastors. When occasion arose for despatch of a congratulatory letter to the nation's first President, it seemed only natural that four laymen sign it along with the Superior. The latter had a keen sense of the difference and newness of the church over which he presided. Unlike missionary churches in the colonies of France, Spain or Portugal, the Catholic Church in the United States had no "metropolitical center" in Europe. The religious climate in which it lived was unique for its freedom from state interference. Church-state separation in the United States was shaped in friendship and co-operation, not, as would be the European case after France's Revolution, in hostility.[19]

Carroll's dreams went significantly unrealized. Tensions—the famous battles with lay trustees—developed even before he became bishop. A more autocratic internal polity resulted. For twenty years until his

death in 1842, Bishop John England tried
in Charleston to gather his church in regu-
lar convention.[20] He also fathered the
series of national councils at Baltimore
which had no parallel elsewhere in the
Latin Church, but the collegiality developed was restricted to a level horizontal
among bishops.[21] Priests grumbled and
laity were excluded.[22] The vertical thrust
withered. More perhaps than other religious groups in America, the Catholic community was subjected to a "colonization"
model, as its several national groups moved
to isolate themselves from one another. A
final and very crucial factor was the tie
American Catholics preserved with a Roman central administration which spent
the century responding to another and
very different revolution, the one which
happened in France.[23] Americans pro-
ceeded collegially and were cool to the
notion of papal infallibility. Rome cen-
tralized and infallibility was defined. Living in a religiously plural atmosphere,
Americans inclined to dialogue. Rome
produced in 1864 the Syllabus of Errors.
American bishops responded with embar-

rassment. The Syllabus did not become part of their "scriptures." When they met in council two years later, its preoccupations were omitted from their agenda.[24] But by that year, 1866, what an Episcopal clergyman had called the "Carrollite" church was gone. With the waves of immigration that reached flood tide after 1830 the American Catholic community came to its first watershed. The colonial-federal style disappeared, to be replaced by a model geared to the needs of a largely alien constituency which helped shatter forever the homogeneity of the eighty-five per cent British-descended people who had made a Revolution and a new nation. The original American Catholics retired to the decent obscurity of St. Mary's and Charles counties in Maryland, to Nelson County in the "Holy Land" of Kentucky and to the Pennsylvania Dutch country, or they melted into America's cities. The age of the immigrants lasted until the second watershed, sometime after World War II, introduced the third and present era in the community's history.[25]

The Immigrants

The main period of American Catholic history, that of the immigrants, has been well picked over, although its definitive story is still to be written.[26] The standard thesis has been that the church served to "Americanize" the immigrant, to fuse Irish, German, Slavic and Italian Catholics in the great melting pot. There are those today, myself among them, with doubts about the melting pot, and recent historians have pointed to severe divisions within the Catholic community. The melting pot, of course, was an Anglo-Saxon model. To the extent that elements in the American Catholic mix refused to become part of the fondue boiling away within it, they were rejecting some share in America's classic self-understanding and myths.

British Dominican Fergus Kerr recently reminded us that we must be conscious of three "churches": the hierarchical, the popular and the academic.[27] The hierarchical has perhaps been badgered and battered enough. Its American style, with blessed exceptions like John Martin Henni, was often set by needs not closely enough aligned with the pastoral function. Inspecting American dioceses for the Vatican in 1878, Irish Bishop George Conroy fastened on problems caused by rapid growth, financial instability occasioned by wildly gyrating boom-and-bust cycles and the need to serve huge numbers of immigrants. The hierarchical church had become an administrative church, where "the most valued gifts [in episcopal candidates —and the same was true of pastors] were properly those of a banker and not of a pastor of souls."[28] The popular church of the immigrant generation did not perhaps revel in sophistication or sound the depths in acquaintance with a tradition now bimillenial, but America's Catholic people preserved and to this day demonstrate a remarkably resilient and authentic sacramental sense. It is on the academic side of the street that, for all its institutions, American Catholicism has been weakest, and this must be of interest to the centennial successors of Fathers Rigge, Cornely and friends.

On whatever level one looks, the panoply of American Catholic education is impressive. It is unique in the whole history of organized Christianity. There is not, and never has been, its equal, at any time, anywhere. But American Catholic schools and the American Catholic intellectual tradition have been largely pedestrian, often doggedly so, and insistently derivative, borrowing by turns from nineteenth-century French thought, and then the rigidly sterile Thomism which came our way in the wake of *Aeterni Patris*.[29] There was the Chesterbelloc moment. The more recent import trade is from France, Germany, Holland and Latin America. All reflections of experiences not our own or at best partially our own. American Catholics of the immigrant period (psychologically hardly ended) have some advantage of Protestant peers in that their rhetoric is not entangled with less memorable aspects of a mutual past. But advantage fades with realization of the American poverty of nearly all the Catholic rhetoric. Is it possibly tied to the fact that in Catholic universities—institutions which for the most part simply "happened" without much planning to colleges opened for the immigrants—theology did not become a really serious discipline until the day before yesterday? It was at Land O'Lakes, Wisconsin, in July, 1968, that for the first time in our history a significant group of Catholic educators acknowledged that our universities should look "first of all and distinctively" to theology to find their identity.[30] A tumultuous thirteen years have followed. With what consequences?

The immigrant saga, for all the problems it bequeaths, is a glorious chapter in American Catholic history. I believe it fulfills the function which Bellah reserved in general United States history for the Revolution: it sums up and represents for us the final act of exodus from Europe. That conflicts with the overall civil religion. But it is where we look for origins, where moods take shape and myths are found. In *Federalist Paper* 2, nearly two centuries ago, John Jay premised his recommendation of the new Constitution on the assumption that:

> Providence has been pleased to give this one
> connected country to one connected people—a
> people descended from the same ancestors,
> speaking the same language, professing the
> same religion, attached to the same principles
> of government, very similar in their manners
> and customs.[31]

That homogeneity ended. The immigrants
ended it. Most of them were not Roman
Catholics. Nine out of forty million were.
They became American Catholicism. In
the popular mind they became identified
with immigration, particularly with its less
savory aspects. Just as "white ethnic" became a codeword in the 1970s, so was "immigrant" a codeword in an earlier generation for the grandparents of those ethnics.

The Last Era

We are chronologically in the third era
of American Catholicism. Exactly when it
began is problematic. Restrictive immigration laws in 1921 and 1924 were a factor.
The hordes of immigrants noted by Bishop
Conroy no longer poured through Ellis
Island, and those who did come were
not so often from Catholic countries. The

Catholic community had time to catch its breath and flex its muscles and it did, with splendiferous displays like Cardinal Mundelein's 1926 Eucharistic Congress in Chicago, complete with cardinal-filled "Red Train" streaking cross country and pontifical masses attracting the faithful by the hundreds of thousands. Not to be outdone, Cardinal Dougherty that same year celebrated the national sesquicentennial in Philadelphia's Municipal Stadium under a baldacchino modeled after the one designed by Bernini for St. Peter's in Rome. An even more fascinating mingling of symbolisms occurred eight years later when Maryland's tercentenary was marked by the military parade into Baltimore's stadium of thousands of habited religious led by the Georgetown University marching band. At the consecration of the mass, sabers flashed, bugles sounded and an artillery salute was fired. The community was handed occasional reminders of its eccentricity—the 1928 election was a difficult time—but both popular and hierarchical religion clearly flourished. The situation of academic religion was not as good. In the integrist aftermath of Modernism, it lay dead in the water.[32]

Events in, around and rising out of the Second World War certainly helped precipitate the third era. Immigrants and their children were integrated into and diffused throughout the population at an accelerated rate. The New Deal, the success of the labor unions, opportunities offered by the 1944 GI Bill of Rights, all contributed substantially to profound change in the makeup, style and possibilities of the Catholic community. By the 1950s, despite Paul Blanshard's best efforts, Catholics were a peaceably accepted fixture on the American landscape. Too peaceably for their own good, thoughtful readers of Will Herberg might feel.[33] The process away from Immigrant Church was well under way. A chain of events was the final catalyst: election in October, 1958, of Angelo Giuseppe Roncalli as Pope John XXIII, John F. Kennedy's election in 1960, the opening two years later of Vatican II, and then that truly catholic, ecumenical, event, the global civic and social turbulence of the late sixties.

The second watershed in American Catholic history, beyond which—no matter how longingly many look back—we have now passed, signaled no gentle, imperceptible, transition. Wherever and however one cares to set the date, the world-wide Christian community, and American Catholics within it, came to and passed through one of those fundamentally revolutionary moments which have been the stuff of Christians' history since a tiny Jewish sect transformed itself into the Gentile church of the Eastern Mediterranean, which in turn became that of the Roman Empire and then of Europe and so, on and on, to the globally catholic Christianity of today. Models shaped in earlier incarnations bear re-thinking. That is true for internal structure, thought-patterns and functioning. It is true for the Catholic community's understanding of and relationship to the world in which it lives.

Today

What does it all have to tell us? What from the past can be of use to interpret the present? How have Catholics understood themselves? How have they understood America? What have been the myths, heroes, events, scriptures, rituals? What religious understandings have prevailed?

Catholics of the colonial-federal era came with the nation. Quietly, solidly and undemonstratively religious, they resonated instinctively as well as deliberately with their political and social surroundings. One has but to read John Carroll's correspondence to realize that a principle of action near the top of his priorities was avoidance of rancor and disharmony. He believed, and acted on it, that leadership in the church demanded thorough grounding in the tradition—personal familiarity with Scripture, the Fathers, Councils, the theologians. His knowledge of the church's past, and personal acquaintance through study with the ideas of those whose religious views differed from his own, enabled him to avoid polemics for the sake of polemics.[34] The colonial-federal group had an advantage. They pre-existed the overwhelming neo-ultramontane tide that engulfed Catholicism in reaction to the

French Revolution and projected on a universal scale European solutions to European problems. At the same time, their
efforts—John Carroll's and John England's
foremost among them—to shape a polity
and a theology Catholic and American
were frustrated by causes internal as well
as external. The real shaping of America's
Catholic community was done differently,
in immigrant days, by the great human
tide of the 1830s and after.

Immigrant Catholic America's heroes
were America's heroes. George Washing-
ton's and Abraham Lincoln's pictures hung
in parochial school classrooms. But there
were other images too: a crucifix, statues
of Our Lady, the saints. Immigrant Catholics had a very living father-image: that of
the pope. It was, though modern Catholics
are incredulous, a phenomenon born in the
nineteenth century, fed by Napoleon's persecution of Pius VI and Pius VII, and by
the travails of Pius IX at the hands of
Garibaldi and Cavour and his ultimate
destiny as "Prisoner of the Vatican." Immigrant Catholics had their own exodus
myth. If they heard in school of Bunker

Hill and Valley Forge and "No taxation
without representation," they knew in their
own flesh and bones of steerage and days
"on the ice" and Ellis Island and "No Irish
need apply." For most, their frontier, that
geographical reality which contributed to
their shaping, was the city. Original America retired to farm and small town and
feared the urban denizens—who in fact
could be quite fearsome. Catholics studied
the Declaration of Independence and the
Constitution, but they had other scriptures
too: the Baltimore Catechism and, filtered
down in one way or other, that relatively
new genre, the papal encyclical. Some, like
Rerum Novarum and *Quadragesimo Anno*,
helped Catholic integration in the chang-
ing socio-economic scene, particularly in
the 1930s. Other papal writings created
problems. When it was being written into
fundamental law, John Carroll had fairly
reveled in the constitutional guarantee of
freedom of religion and separation be-
tween state and church. A century and a
half later, that great social progressive
John A. Ryan could not find his way out
of Leo XIII's contrary views.[35] John Court-

ney Murray arrived only as the immigrant
period ended.

Catholics celebrated civic holidays, but
in self-consciously non-religious fashion.
They had their own holidays, spelled with
a "y" instead of an "i," a peculiar list not-
able for having no discernible raison d'être
in the American Catholic past, but tena-
ciously held on to. Days of feast and fast
and of abstinence were ritually kept, often
at some personal cost, and borne as a
badge of honor. There were awkward moments. Immigrant Catholics did not reso-
nate easily with American moralizers—pro-
hibitionists, abolitionists, promoters of the
Puritan Sunday. The reasons were complex
and not wholly to their discredit. Common
schools were another sore point. The public school did not come with the republic,
but many acted as if it did. With Justice
Felix Frankfurter, they took it as "a sym-
bol of our secular unity."[36] Catholics dis-
sented. They had gone their own uniquely
American route of the common parish
school, and they remembered only too well
the curiously mixed signals sent them in
Nativist days—days also of Evangelical

Empire—in the accusation that they were greedy of public funds for "sectarian schools," whose crime was that in them "neither the Sacred Scriptures, nor any portions of them, are read."[37] Immigrant Catholics knew American symbols well; they measured them by another set all their own.

In a Global World

If the church of the immigrants suffered from defects inherent in its constituency and make-up, its accomplishment still was simply staggering. Today's challenge is to achievements analogously as successful. New symbols, new rhetoric—and the disappearance of some or much of the old— must be taken for granted. The church, conscious of itself as People of God, will find its orientations conditioned by the contemporary humanness of its own community and by the needs of the other actual human beings with whom in pilgrimage it shares the planet and beyond. That course was set fifteen years ago when *Gaudium et Spes* proclaimed that "the joy and hope, the grief and anguish" of

modern humanity were those equally of
Christ's followers.[38] This university, so long
as it wishes to extend its centenary use of
the word "Jesuit," must attend to the man-
date of the Thirty-Second Jesuit Congregation in 1975 and engage in "the struggle
for faith and that struggle for justice which
it includes."[39]

The challenge is multiple. National images and symbols must yield in the ideal
order, and increasingly and effectively in
the real order, to global concerns. Denis
O'Connell's American Catholic era is over,
if indeed it ever really dominated. Catholicism must dissociate itself from the American civil religion insofar as that means
narrow nationalist identification of the
Kingdom with the nation's political aims.
Liberation and repression of it are, everywhere, everyone's problem. Religious toleration must develop into substantive ecu-
menism that explores every avenue to pool
religious resources in the common cause
of humanity, and among Christians explores every avenue by which we may
become one. Equality is a very American
word, one which Tocqueville associated

particularly with American Catholics. What of that boast today? Racial equality, and the full partnership of women in our society and in our church, are far from achievement. What instead are the concerns which even the most casual observer identifies as "Catholic?" Can we state an authentically Christian, as opposed to a baptized Stoic, understanding of marriage and married love, and of human sexuality in all its aspects? To what extent are we simply-swept along on prevailing cultural winds? Or, on the other hand, to what extent do we insist on responding to cultural needs long since exhausted? Have we set aside our prophetic vocation and been content to be morals police force and baptizers of civil polity?

The agenda is a full one for the Catholic Church in America in its popular, hierarchical and academic elements. Christendom is no more. Neither medieval Catholic nor nineteenth-century American Protestant. We live in a secular America in a secular world. Some in the face of that fold their tents and slip quietly away. Others react by circling the wagons. There is an alternative: fresh appropriation of the tradition as we sound new depths in living with the tension and conflict endemic to a world in change. That is the Catholic way; it has both vertical and horizontal dimensions. Our approach can be shaped neither by the parochial "universalism" of a church really European nor by continued rote response to needs of immigrant ancestors which are not our needs. If we would be Catholic, we must be acutely conscious of, and at the same time really freed from, both the glories and the miscues of the past. Tradition is Catholic when it is active, helpful and contemporary; not when it is passive, archaic and restrictive.

Catholics sought in America the Promised Land of the Saints, a land of promise and of sanctuary. They made themselves tolerably comfortable, and often a good deal more than that, in the God's New Israel of the Puritans, the secular home of Manifest Destiny. But a late twentieth-century vision must include more than the evening-world on the western horizon toward which they sailed. The time has come to haul ourselves back into Brendan's wicker basket and search out newer worlds. I expect there will be the occasional friendly Jasconius along the way, and certainly some of poor Judas's little volcanic devils. Perhaps there will be a delightful island of hospitable monks, if not of Latin-speaking choir-birds. Strange talk, isn't it? The imagery of Star Trek is better suited to our future than that of Brendan the Abbot. The earth has become in our own lifetimes, for the first time in its multi-millenial existence, self-consciously global and is in fact poised on the edge of the interplanetary. The world, the United States, its Catholic community—and Marquette University—have all come an extraordinary way since an early September morning in 1881. Father Rigge and Father Cornely, the three scholastics, Father Lalumiere and Bishop Henni could scarcely in their wildest dreams have imagined what we know to be fact about the century that divides us. It has been good to know their world, civil and religious, and to appreciate its symbols, so respondent to its needs. Now we have our

own agenda, our own needs. I wonder
how the Pere Marquette lecturer who
stands here in the year 2081 will reflect
on what we have done to respond to them!

NOTES

1. Raphael N. Hamilton, S.J., *The Story of Marquette University* (Milwaukee, 1953).

2. Herbert C. Noonan, S.J., "The Need of Jesuit Universities," *Woodstock Letters,* 54 (1924), 238-248.

3. Hamilton, p. 8.

4. Peter Leo Johnson, *Crosier on the Frontier: The Life of John Martin Henni* (Madison, 1959).

5. Martin E. Marty, *Righteous Empire: The Protestant Experience in America* (New York, 1970); H. Richard Niebuhr, *The Kingdom of God in America* (New York, 1937); Conrad Cherry, ed., *God's New Israel: Religious Interpretations of America's Destiny* (Englewood Cliffs, 1971); Robert T. Handy, *A Christian America: Protestant Hopes and Historical Realities* (New York, 1971); Sidney E. Mead, *The Nation with the Soul of a Church* (New York, 1975); *Winthrop Papers,* II (Boston, 1931), p. 295.

6. Samuel E. Morison, *The European Discovery of America: The Northern Voyages, A.D. 500-1600* (New York, 1971), pp. 13-31.

7. Handy, p. 213.

8. Alexis de Tocqueville, *Democracy in America* (2 vols.; ed. Phillips Bradley; New York, 1945), 1:311.

9. Philip Schaff, *America: A Sketch of Its Political, Social and Religious Character* (ed. Perry Miller; Cambridge MA, 1961), P. 88.

10. Dorothy Dohen, *Nationalism and American Catholicism* (New York, 1967).

11. Robert N. Bellah, "Civil Religion in America," in William G. McLoughlin and Robert N. Bellah, eds., *Religion in America* (Boston, 1968), pp. 20, 14.

12. Mary L. Schneider, "A Catholic Perspective on American Civil Religion," in Thomas M. McFadden, ed., *America in Theological Perspective* (New York, 1976), pp. 123-139.

13. John Courtney Murray, S.J., *We Hold These Truths: Catholic Reflections on the American Proposition* (New York, 1960), p. 42.

14. Hugh J. Nolan, ed., *Pastoral Letters of the American Hierarchy, 1792-1970* (Huntington, 1971), p. 167. See Isaac Hecker, *Aspirations of Nature* (New York, 1857); *id., Questions of the Soul* (New York, 1859).

15. Gerald P. Fogarty, S.J., *The Vatican and the Americanist Crisis: Denis J. O'Connell, American Agent in Rome, 1885-1903* (Rome, 1974), p. 280.

16. Joseph F. Gower and Richard M. Leliaert, O.S.C., eds., *The Brownson-Hecker Correspondence* (Notre Dame, 1979), p. 142.

17. William A. Clebsch, *American Religious Thought: A History* (Chicago, 1973), p. 114.

18. Robert N. Bellah, *The Broken Covenant: American Civil Religion in a Time of Trial* (New York, 1975), p. 2.

19. The best way to know John Carroll is to read in Thomas O'Brien Hanley, S.J., ed., *The John Carroll Papers* (3 vols.; Notre Dame, 1976).

20. Ignatius Reynolds, ed., *The Works of the Right Rev. John England, First Bishop of Charleston* (5 vols.; Baltimore, 1845), 5:91-108.

21. Eugenio Corecco, *La Formazione della Chiesa Cattolica negli Stati Uniti d'America attraverso l'attività sinodale* (Brescia, 1970); James Hennesey, S.J., "The Baltimore Conciliar Tradition," *Annuarium Historiae Conciliorum*, 3 (1971), 71-88.

22. Robert Trisco, "Bishops and Their Priests in the United States," in John Tracy Ellis, ed., *The Catholic Priest in the United States: Historical Investigations* (Collegeville, 1971), pp. 111-292.

23. Derek Holmes, *The Triumph of the Holy See: A Short History of the Papacy in the Nineteenth Century* (London/Shepherdstown, 1978); James Hennesey, S.J., "Catholic and Roman: The Church before Lumen Gentium," *Emmanuel*, 85 (1979), 485-494.

24. *Idem*, "The Baltimore Council of 1866: An American Syllabus," *Records of the American Catholic Historical Society of Philadelphia* [RACHS], 77 (1966), 175-189.

25. *Idem*, "Square Peg in a Round Hole: On Being Roman Catholic in America," *RACHS*, 84 (1973), 167-195.

26. Jay P. Dolan, *The Immigrant Church: New York's Irish and German Catholics, 1815-1865* (Baltimore, 1975); Silvano Tomasi and M. Engels, eds., *The Italian Experience in the United States* (Staten Island, 1970); Keith P. Dyrud *et al.*, *The Other Catholics* (New York, 1978); Anthony J. Kuzniewski, S.J., *Faith and Fatherland: The Polish Church War in Wisconsin 1896-1908* (Notre Dame, 1980).

27. Fergus Kerr, O.P., "Rahner Retrospective I—Rupturing Der Pianische Monolithismus," *New Blackfriars*, 61 (1980), 227, commenting on Newman's 1877 preface to *Lectures on the Prophetic Office*.

28. George Conroy, "Relazione sullo stato presente della Chiesa Cattolica negli Stati Uniti d'America," Archives of the Sacred Congregation for Propagation of the Faith, Rome, Congressi, America Centrale, 36 (1882), fol. 197.

29. James Hennesey, S.J., "Leo XIII's Thomistic Revival: A Political and Philosophical Event," *Journal of Religion*, 58 (1978), S185-S197; Gerald A. McCool, S.J., *Catholic Theology in the Nineteenth Century: The Quest for a Unitary Method* (New York, 1977).

30. "The Catholic University of Today," *America*, August 12, 1968, pp. 154-156.

31. *The Federalist* (ed. Jacob E. Cooke; Middletown CT, 1961), p. 9.

32. William H. Halsey, *The Survival of American Innocence: Catholicism in an Era of Disillusionment, 1920-1940* (Notre Dame, 1980).

33. Will Herberg, *Protestant, Catholic, Jew: An Essay in American Religious Sociology* (Garden City, 1955).

34. James Hennesey, S.J., "An Eighteenth Century Bishop: John Carroll of Baltimore," *Archivum Historiae Pontificiae,* 16 (1978), 171-204; *idem.,* "The Vision of John Carroll," *Thought,* 54 (1979), 322-333; *idem,* "John Carroll: American Bishop," *New Catholic World,* 223 (1980), 225-227.

35. John A. Ryan and Moorhouse I.X. Millar, S.J., *The State and the Church* (New York, 1922).

36. See Frankfurter's concurring opinion in the 1948 McCollum case, in Joseph E. Blau, ed., *Cornerstones of Religious Freedom in America* (New York, 1964), p. 262.

37. Robert Baird, *Religion in America* (London, 1844; ed. Henry Warner Bowden; New York, 1970), p. 261.

38. Austin Flannery, O.P., ed., *Vatican Council II: The Conciliar and Post Conciliar Documents* (Collegeville, 1975), p. 903.

39. John W. Padberg, S.J., ed., *Documents of the 31st and 32nd General Congregations of the Society of Jesus* (St. Louis, 1977), p. 401.

The Perè Marquette Theology Lectures

1969: "The Authority for Authority,"
by Quentin Quesnell
Professor of Theology at
Marquette University

1970: "Mystery and Truth,"
by John Macquarrie
Professor of Theology at
Union Theology Seminary, New York

1971: "Doctrinal Pluralism,"
by Bernard Lonergan, S.J.
Professor of Theology at
Regis College, Ontario

1972: "Infallibility,"
by George A. Lindbeck
Professor of Theology at
Yale University

1973: "Ambiguity in Moral Choice,"
by Richard A. McCormick, S.J.
Professor of Moral Theology at
Bellarmine School of Theology

1974: "Church Membership as a Catholic
and Ecumenical Problem,"
by Avery Dulles, S.J.
Professor of Theology at
Woodstock College

1975: "The Contributions of Theology to
Medical Ethics,"
by James Gustafson
University Professor of Theological Ethics at
University of Chicago

1976: "Religious Values in an Age of Violence,"
by Rabbi Marc Tanenbaum
Director of National Interreligious Affairs
American Jewish Committee, New York City

1977: "Truth Beyond Relativism: Karl Mannheim's
Sociology of Knowledge,"
by Gregory Baum
Professor of Theology and Religious Studies at
St. Michael's College

1978: "A Theology of 'Uncreated Energies'"
by George A. Maloney, S.J.
Professor of Theology
John XXIII Center For Eastern Christian Studies
Fordham University

1980: "Method in Theology: An Organon For
Our Time"
by Frederick E. Crowe, S.J.
Research Professor in Theology
Regis College, Toronto

1981: "Catholics in the Promised Land of
the Saints
by James Hennesey, S.J.
Professor of the History of Christianity
Boston College

Copies of this lecture and the others in the series are
obtainable from:

Marquette University Press
Marquette University
Milwaukee, Wisconsin 53233
USA

DATE DUE
